Who cleans the streets?

Written by Barbara MacKay

Illustrated by Mark Ruffle

Collins

Who's in this book?

Listen and say

Download the audio at www.collins.co.uk/839781

Dan

Grace

Bill

Joe

🎧 Holly and Mark are going to school. Holly says, "Oh no, the street is dirty."

Mark asks, "Who cleans
the streets, Mum?"

This is Bill. He cleans the streets in his small truck.

small truck

The truck has got two small brushes.
The brushes clean the streets.

brush

Bill's truck cleans big streets.

It cleans small streets, too!

Bill wears white and yellow trousers.
He's got big boots.

Bill has got a brush, too. He cleans between the cars.

Grace and Dan are in town. Grace is driving the truck.

street bins

Dan is taking the rubbish out of the black street bins.

Dan and Grace are in Park Street.
There are lots of bins here.

Park Street

Park Street is clean now!

Joe's big truck cleans the big streets.
There's a lot of water!

big truck

Joe's truck can clean this.
His truck has got lots of big brushes.

Joe is stopping his truck. There's a frog in the street.

What's he doing?
That's good, Joe.

It's the end of the day.

The streets are clean now.

Picture dictionary

Listen and repeat

bin

brush

clean

dirty

rubbish

truck

1 Look and match

Grace and Dan

Bill

Joe

2 Listen and say

Collins

Published by Collins
An imprint of HarperCollins*Publishers*
Westerhill Road
Bishopbriggs
Glasgow
G64 2QT

HarperCollins*Publishers*
Macken House, 39/40 Mayor Street Upper,
Dublin 1
DO1 C9W8
Ireland

William Collins' dream of knowledge for all began with the publication of his first book in 1819.

A self-educated mill worker, he not only enriched millions of lives, but also founded a flourishing publishing house. Today, staying true to this spirit, Collins books are packed with inspiration, innovation and practical expertise. They place you at the centre of a world of possibility and give you exactly what you need to explore it.

10 9 8 7 6 5 4 3

ISBN 978-0-00-839781-4

Collins® and COBUILD® are registered trademarks of HarperCollins*Publishers* Limited

www.collins.co.uk/elt

British Library Cataloguing in Publication Data

A catalogue record for this publication is available from the British Library.

Author: Barbara MacKay
Illustrator: Mark Ruffle (Beehive)
Series editor: Rebecca Adlard
Commissioning editor: Zoë Clarke
Publishing manager: Lisa Todd
Product managers: Jennifer Hall and Caroline Green
In-house editor: Alma Puts Keren
Project manager: Emily Hooton
Editor: Emma Wilkinson
Proofreaders: Natalie Murray and Michael Lamb
Cover designer: Kevin Robbins
Typesetter: 2Hoots Publishing Services Ltd
Audio produced by id audio, London
Reading guide author: Emma Wilkinson
Production controller: Rachel Weaver
Printed and bound in the UK by Pureprint

MIX
Paper | Supporting responsible forestry
FSC
www.fsc.org
FSC™ C007454

This book contains FSC™ certified paper and other controlled sources to ensure responsible forest management.

For more information visit: www.harpercollins.co.uk/green

Download the audio for this book and a reading guide for parents and teachers at www.collins.co.uk/839781